Stop
Choose
Change

Thriving and Surviving
Tough Times

DIANA CUSHWAY

ISBN: 1544900007
ISBN-13: 978-1544900001

DEDICATION

This book is dedicated to my amazing husband

Bill Evans.

"By recalling the past and freezing the present he could open up the gates of time and through them see all allegedly sequential things as a single masterwork with neither boundaries nor divisions... he did know, beginning long before he could express it, that when the gates of time were thrown open, the world was saturated with love"

- Mark Helprin
Sunlight and Shadows

"I think my favorite part of Antarctica is just looking out." "You know why?" Dad asked. "When your eyes are softly focused on the horizon for sustained periods, your brain releases endorphins. It's the same as a runner's high. These days, we all spend our lives staring at screens twelve inches in front of us. It's a nice change."

- Maria Semple
Where'd You Go Bernadette

"Everything in the Universe is constantly changing, and nothing stays the same, and we must understand how quickly time flows by if we are to wake up and truly live our lives."

- Ruth Ozeki
A Tale for the Time Being

About this Book

This book tells the story of how I decided to take the reins of both my illness and my life and my cure. At the end of each chapter, I include some simple, fast, and easy to use strategies that you can practice and implement in just a few minutes a day. It is only by constant practice that you can redirect your life and keep redirecting it. These activities can change and enhance your body/brain physiology. There is so much exciting new research about our brains' neuroplasticity. We have the ability to rewire our reaction to stimuli. We can choose to weigh options slowly and develop healthy reactions instead of reacting impulsively with our fight-or-flight response.

I developed some of these activities through a lifetime of reading about exercise, meditation, spiritual practice, quantum physics, prayer, breath work, and other challenging topics. However, if you want to incorporate them into your daily life and achieve results, you have to do the work; the key is practice, study and repetition. I believe there are many roads to immersing oneself in the awe of the universe/multiverse. Whatever road you choose is what I call "plugging in" and connecting to life. These strategies can help you get through the hardest days of your life. I hope you will come to realize you are not alone.

MY STORY

My story actually begins when I decided to walk away from a tenured position with full benefits as head of the Dance Program at Skyline College in San Bruno, California. For several years, I had been working in a frustrating situation where promises were not kept. I was working crazy hours, doing a lot of paperwork and fund raising, which did not leave time for creativity. At the same time, an elderly aunt with senile dementia was living with me, and my sister-in-law was struggling with brain cancer while trying to raise her young daughter. My husband finally said, "You cannot continue working under these conditions for this crazy guy. You need to get out." I realized my husband was right on one level, but on another I knew that this was the job I had always wanted. Being a dancer, choreographer, director, and professor was my identity. And yet, I decided to quit the full-time position with all of the politics and paperwork, deciding instead to continue to teach classes but stay away from the craziness. This decision forced me to grow in new ways and was the best thing I could have done for myself, considering what was to come.

I have no regrets about my decision. I finally had time to be with and take care of family. Ironically, soon after I left, the "dysfunctional guy" was replaced by an utterly fantastic person. Had I known this, I never would have left the full-time position. If I hadn't left, I never would have had the time to change and do the soul-searching that helped me with upcoming events.

Soon after, I lost five beloved friends within a four-month time frame. Among these, my friend, colleague and collaborator of many years died suddenly of a heart attack, my sister-in-law died shortly after, and my beloved "mother"/aunt died 2 ½ months later. The loss, grief and life-altering upheaval precipitated changes in me that challenged my preconceived notions of who I thought I was and what I should be doing with my life. No longer did I feel the need to impress with titles, skills or accomplishments. (Well, most of the time. However, I have to keep working on this too!)

I broke the definition of "me" down with mind-changing results. This transitional moment when I dropped many of my preconceived definitions of myself rocked my world. As my internal definition of self-concept shifted, I realized that by opening up to different possibilities, there were now an infinite number of doors and windows available to me. (Now, when people ask me what I do, I tell them, I am just working on " being" not doing). I wanted to share my strategies so that others could unlock their own doors and windows to discover their own healing potential, but it wasn't until later, after the strategies stood a test by fire, that I knew I had to write this book.

My journey to write started in the spring of 2012 with back pain so intense it felt like an electrocution. Doctors had no clue what it was, but prescribed heavy painkillers and said, "Let's wait and see." By summer, I was lying all day on the floor of my isolated Sierra Nevada mountain cabin with my calves up on a chair. I put the bottle of painkillers on my kitchen counter and told myself, "Okay, Diana, you can take one of these pills any time you want; however, if you block your symptoms, you won't discover what is aggravating your back or exacerbating the problem." My reward, if I could make it through the day without the pills, was a glass of wine at day's end.

Because mindfulness has long been a part of my life and my college lectures, and because this particular summer provided me with an abundance of time, I intensified my 25-year study and began to devour neuroscience, meditation, and stress reduction books in my search for a cure. I spent numerous hours reading, meditating, working with loving-kindness, and experimenting with all types of breath work. Eventually, I came to a place of total surrender, realizing that it was possible that I would never again be able to sit up in a car let alone teach dance classes. I was resolved that I could accept that outcome if I could just have fifteen minutes at the end of my day to at least stand up and absorb the beauty of the planet. When I told my husband all that I was learning, he said, "You really get this stuff. You're teaching it to me, so maybe you should do something with it." That is when, lying on my back with a magic marker and a legal notepad, I started to write. The result turned out to be the *Stress Management* class that I taught the following spring semester at Skyline College. That class became the foundation for this book.

Late in the summer, I had a conversation with a doctor from a small clinic in the Sierra Mountains who told me that my back problem might be structural. I thought perhaps he was right and delved into a new journey using my aunt's old anatomy books which happened to be at the cabin. As I read, I remembered that due to an old college injury, I had stopped stretching my right hamstring after teaching my dance classes. Perhaps I was out of balance and torqueing my pelvis when I moved. By studying the books, I identified the muscles I needed to stretch to possibly fix the problem. To honor my plan, I even wrote out a mock doctor's prescription delineating my physical therapy for the next few weeks. Using my prescription, I stretched and worked my muscles throughout the day. Three weeks later, I was back at school, with zero back pain, teaching an intense cardio dance class.

What could have been a happy ending wasn't, however. Though, in retrospect, perhaps it prepared me for the biggest fight of my life. One year later, I was diagnosed with cancer: not one, but two. I had cancer in my uterus, and in my fallopian tube, I had a particularly rare and ravaging type called serous carcinoma. I quickly underwent three surgeries followed by four months of chemotherapy.

To get through the ensuing months, I chose to draw on the knowledge I had gained through my back injury, the latest information I researched about the neuroplasticity of the brain, and deliberately chose how I would approach each day of treatment. I called it, "becoming a superpower with flaws."

I was passionately driven to write

because people kept asking me to share my ideas on how to cope with unimaginable hardship. I wish I had read this book when I was going through my struggles, but I had to make that journey in order to be the person telling the story today. It is my sincere hope that when you read this, you will find something that can be of help to you.

THE POWER OF MINDFULNESS

I am passionate about staying fit in mind, body and spirit. However, as a high energy person, I have two switches: on and off. I knew that I needed to find a middle switch and slower speeds in my approaches to life. The first book that I worked with intensively was Jon Kabbat- Zinn's, *Wherever You Go There You Are (Mindfulness Meditation in Everyday Life)*. I would finish the book's exercises, then restart from the very beginning and do them all over again. Another book that I studied and reread was *The Issue at Hand: Essays on Buddhist Mindfulness Practice* by Gil Fronsdal.

I also recommend *Buddha's Brain* by Rick Hanson, PhD with Richard Mendius, MD. Additionally, for two and half years I worked and reworked the Steps of Tao, utilizing Dr. Wayne W. Dyer's book *Change Your Thoughts - Change Your Life: Living the Wisdom of the Tao*. Through these readings, I found that deep breathing and mindfulness work were the only way to slow me down. Not only has this discipline given me a better quality of life, but I am positive it actually saved my life several times this past year.

Using a holistic approach to all my teaching, I discovered how much this training helped my students as they struggled with job, family and work. Students still contact me about how lectures, classes and individual discussions impacted their lives. I remember one young man from China taking my Stress Management class. He had gone to top notch schools, was fluent in at least five languages, and felt stuck at Skyline when a perceptive counselor placed him in my class. He resented everything I said and resisted every exercise. To him, mindfulness and meditation were frivolous thinking and an incredible waste of his time. He refused to work on a journal or utilize my suggestions for reflective writing or even drawing. Finally, I met with him after class, trying to find a way to break through. That was when I found out the stress level in his life. He was not only worried about the pressure to get accepted into top schools, but his girlfriend had also recently moved elsewhere for a job. In addition, he had just been in a car accident. He said he was so frustrated that when he went home at night he kicked his dog. Ouch! Obviously, he felt guilty about his coping mechanisms which just intensified the negative behavior.

Gradually, I convinced him to channel his anger into a journal. He ended up setting fire to a few pages (literally), duct-taping a whole page, and putting safety pins in another;

it was great! He told me he had stopped kicking his poor little dog and was working on reframing his thinking and view of the world. It was exciting to see his dawning "awareness' of the benefits of journaling, slowing down, and being mindful in his day to day life. He smiled more, interacted with the other students instead of isolating himself, and applied himself to working hard to achieve his goals. He found other ways to think, feel, and process and was no longer trapped in a rigid mindset. His final exam was to give a presentation about a book by Eckhart Tolle to a class of forty female students. He delivered an insightful sixty-minute lecture on mindfulness and how it applied to his life, followed by a student question/answer session in which he demonstrated his thorough grasp of the material. He emailed me that summer and told me he was admitted to three top level schools. He chose U. C. Berkeley.

My passion for sharing the power of

mindfulness extends beyond the classroom. One day while I was at the hospital for a chemo treatment, with various needles hanging out of my arm, I observed a young woman with similar needles looking at them every few seconds, clearly distressed. I watched her for a while and decided to approach. I told her I thought I could help her get through the day if she wanted my help. She acquiesced, and we started breath work. I kept it simple, telling her to put her hands on her belly and just feel it expand and collapse like a balloon. Then I asked her to pay attention to the air coming in and out of her nose. Eventually, we progressed to mindfulness. I had her tell me what she liked about the room, what she saw in the sky, and what was beautiful about the day outside. I concluded with loving-kindness, asking her about her family members and who was most important to her. As we moved through the exercises, her face and body language changed. She stopped focusing on the needles, the muscles around her eyes and mouth softened, and she really made eye contact. When the nurse came to get her, the young woman walked out slowly staring back at me.

Shortly after, another patient waiting for a scan came up and congratulated me on the "good thing" I had done to help this young woman. It turned out he was getting a Doctorate in Neuroscience, and we enthusiastically talked about the benefits of mindfulness and all of the new research on ways to "reboot" the brain, to reframe one's thinking.

Another episode that demonstrates the importance of breath work occurred when I was coming out of the anesthesia after one of my surgeries. My body was shaking uncontrollably, so I worked with my breathing. Suddenly, the attending nurse exclaimed, "I don't know what you are doing, but it's working. Your blood pressure and resting heart rate are dropping." I surprised each of my nurses with how quickly I recovered from each procedure and accompanying anesthesia. I was soon alert in the recovery room, and they would comment on my energy and healthy skin tone. In one recovery room, I even worked with my attending nurse, teaching her breath work to deal with the stress of surgical nursing! I firmly believe that attention to exercise, mindfulness techniques and breath work results in faster, positive recoveries.

Mindful Brain Reboots

Before starting each "reboot," take a deep breath, close your eyes, and visualize a stop sign or yellow flashing lights (whatever works for you). Then go over the new reboot. Open your eyes, and start the life changes you want to make. Remember you have to rewrite-rewire your own script. Decide WHO is driving. Practice sitting in the driver's seat, not tossing around in the back of the bus.

- Stuck in traffic? REBOOT! Through your nose, inhale a full belly breath of imaginary garden flowers or the real aromas of a nearby bakery shop. Slowly exhale without straining. Wait to breathe in (feel that pause). Your body will naturally begin the next inhalation. Replace fingers gently on the steering wheel, and slide shoulders down into your back pockets. Keep practicing. You have plenty of time to work on this.

- The brain only fills images of the world around you in rough sketches. Otherwise, you would be overwhelmed with too much data. When you STOP and focus your attention, the mind-eye connection fully fills in the "picture" with stunning detail. Be in that moment.

- Rushing around? Your thoughts swirling and going too fast? STOP! Focus on the sky, bird sounds, the sunset, a pretty blue sweater. Focusing on the sky lifts my attention UP and out of my thoughts, instantly grounding me and uplifting me at the same time. Gather the big reward of being mindfully present.

- Still can't slow down at end of your day? Feel the bottom of your feet as you walk from room to room, slow down your pace, and add belly breath. Try to do this several times throughout your evening.

- Become mindful and grateful of EVERYTHING this earth gives you. It is a privilege to be here.

- Do not fret about not being mindfully present all the time in your life. Focus on the reward when you come back! STOP. Breathe, and with a big compassionate smile say, "Welcome back! I am present and aware." Every time you catch yourself stuck in your thoughts. Don't chastise yourself. Just be happy that you are back and conscious.

- Thoughts are not reality. Come BACK to life around you- now that's real!

- Here's a silly but powerful exercise you can try. I had watched a show with Deepak Chopra talking about his life's work with meditation. I was struck by his claim that since he started meditating nothing bothered him anymore. Try a Chopra Hour where you step into Mr. Chopra's shoes. Buy (costume shop) big black glasses like the ones he wears or imagine wearing a pair. Take on his calm demeanor, and practice not letting anything bother you for one whole hour, then one whole morning, then one whole day.

- Stop! Take two deep breaths to slow down and focus. Then add with subsequent breaths, I am: safe, well, happy, peaceful and at ease. I always add something I want to work on in my life too. Look at something beautiful, giving yourself time to observe.

- I have noticed myself and friends get trapped in "thought-loops," not focused mindfully on the present. Do you see yourself in any of these examples?

- A friend of mine constantly complained about how poorly her boyfriend treated her. I told her I had better use for her time and asked if she was near a wall. She said she was, so I told her to stand in front of it. She stated, "Okay, I am standing in front of the wall." Then I told her to just bang her head against it since that was as effective as going out with this guy and then complaining, ALL THE TIME. Not only did he not deserve her love, he didn't deserve to take her attention away from living on this lovely planet! By the way, she is now married to a wonderful man who cooks fabulous meals for her.

- Another friend was recently reunited with the love of her life, 40 years after they had broken up. This man was obviously still crazy about her, but she couldn't enjoy and accept it because she kept thinking about all of his past girlfriends. I told her how much he obviously loved her. Then I asked her to go find a wall and... (see paragraph above). I said, "When you are done banging your head, think about really living in the life you have right now!"

- Another time her comment was, "When I have "blank," then I will really be happy." It is not "when." It is right now! Find a: thought, image, creature that makes you happy now, right now.

- STOP! Do you really WANT to be in this loop today? CHOOSE your next thought; be present to something around you. Wake up!

- Spider webs sparkling with dew are a gift! Investigate life around you like a child. Don't live like a vampire, heedless of passing time.

- Stop! Take three breaths. Know you can always choose a different fork in the road if you stop, breathe and listen to your body

- The answers are pretty much all inside you, but you will have to get quiet enough to listen. When you become a good friend to yourself, you will be an even better friend to others.

- Did you hear the birds sing today? Were you aware of how the sky looked tonight? Observe the magnificence of the clouds, moon, and sky. Close your eyes and observe the magnificence of yourself. You are made of the stuff of stars.

- When sitting down to a meal, pay attention. Relax your shoulders, or as my friend Cindy says, "slide your shoulders down to your back pockets," sit up straight, look at the table and what food is before you. Set a utensil or glass down slowly. Appreciate the food. If you catch yourself gobbling and hurrying, stop, reboot, and start mindful appreciation over again, thereby cultivating good habits and good digestion in addition to muscle memory.

- Talk to a trusted friend: Slow down the tempo of your speech, pay attention to your breath and deep breathe. Imagine "sliding your shoulders into your back pockets," and don't interrupt.

- I designed this exercise when I first left my full-time Dance position and felt disconnected from the world around me. I would go to a park, focus on some aspect of nature as intently as if I were trying to draw it, and say to myself: I am part of that tree and that tree is part of me. I am part of the sky, cloud, pebble, small ant, leaf, and it is part of me. I practiced this for several years and felt a change, plugged in and not alone.

Mindful Breathing

With mindful breathing, our body tunes IN, slows down and cues the nervous system to calm down. You can reconnect with gratitude for what is around or inside of you when you SLOW down and breathe as you plug into the universe.

A friend, Ellen, once demonstrated to me how to get a full breath. As an educator and voice professional, she has to train people not to use unnecessary muscle tension to breathe. Rather than taking in a stressful breath that sounds like Darth Vader on steroids, imagine instead you are inhaling the delicious scent of bakery goods or flowers in a garden shop. This way you are not forcing in the air and allow the breath to fill your lungs easily. By doing this, you can actually feel your rib cage expand laterally, allowing you to take in more air.

Remember that mindful breathing can help you in many situations. When a person ahead of you in the grocery store line has 16 items instead of the stated twelve, for example. Or you can use it to slow down a distressed person or child. They will respond to your breathing. Practice anywhere, anytime, but practice. I usually do two deep breaths to get myself focused then I continue with five to six very focused breaths to calm down and reset my brain-body. Work longer if you are greatly distressed. Oxygen is FREE! Use it gratefully!

Breathing Exercises

- Imagine inhaling a pleasing, soothing scent. Place hands on belly/chest. Feel your belly rise and fall for two minutes. (Don't have two minutes? Then do it in one.) Inhale through the nose feeling your belly rise, count to 4, hold breath for 16, exhale through the mouth for 8 counts. Practice breath work exercises to relax or energize your body! 16 counts are important to activate your lymphatic system and fully oxygenate your blood. Many people feel tired all the time because they are breathing shallowly in their chest and their bodies are starving for oxygen.

- Revisit your breath work going deeper by engaging awareness of the body parts involved in deep breathing. Feel the belly, chest, nose, and mouth. Pay attention to other parts of your body, feel your feet on the floor, your rear end in your chair, and where possible, lengthen the duration of each exercise.

- Place the tongue behind the front teeth and press. Keep it there for the duration of the exercise. Breathe in for four counts, hold seven counts, exhale eight counts. Breath in and out through your mouth, making a "th" sound. (I read about this exercise in a magazine, but recently found out that this is an exercise created by Dr. Andrew Weil. This is also the exercise I used to stop shaking after anesthesia and after rigors from blood sepsis poisoning.)

- Inhale through the nose and scrunch your face seven counts. Exhale through nose. Relax and breathe in and out for 20 counts (Good for migraines).

- Take a deep breath, pause, and notice how still you are in that pause; add another breath, pause, add a third breath and slowly exhale, feeling the deliciousness of that exhale. Pay attention to the space and quietness in each pause. The slowness of your exhalation engages the relaxation phase of your autonomic nervous system. Use it to calm yourself down.

- Simplest exercise ever: Inhale, exhale (count one) inhale, exhale (count two) Remember to belly breathe and enjoy the delicious miracle of breathing. Lose track? Start from the beginning. Do this for 10 seconds or longer.

- Walk and breathe: Inhale for four counts, exhale for four counts. Play with slowing down each inhale and exhale without tensing your body. This is great if you are walking to class at exam time!

ALTERING TIME

Using mindfulness and altering your perspective of time can be life changing. Time is not necessarily linear, and we can alter time with our thoughts and attitudes. If you experiment with altering your "time perception," you can challenge and change your day, hour, or minute with positive results.

For a year, I set the clock by my bed forward by about an hour, keeping all the rest of my time devices accurate. The result was I would wake up in the morning, after a nap or reading, look at my dresser clock and think,

"Oh no, I've run out of time! I have to hurry and go, go, go!" My subsequent thought would be, "WOW, I have 60 whole minutes before I have to leave for the day." It was glorious, and I decided to change my thinking of time, my thoughts about time, and the internal pressure that could be released through this new thought process.

I played with time before my weekly chemo sessions. I would wake up in the morning and focus on the beauty of the sky, then "time jump" in my mind to a happy activity I had planned in the days ahead. When I arrived for chemo, I would stay present and flood myself with gratitude for the incredible hardworking nurses that I was so lucky to have caring for me. Listening to my body as I received a chemo infusion one day, I noticed how instantly I felt calmer and soothed when I heard Nurse Practitioner Natasha Curry's voice as she made her rounds. I sat in the infusion chair focused on her presence and my upcoming plans, not the chemo.

Every third week (Wednesday), I received another type of chemo on top of my usual dose. Thursdays I received energy from prednisone, so on Wednesdays I thought about how I would feel the next day, "time jumping" in my mind. On Sundays the effects of the chemo had lessened, and I knew I had at least an hour and a half where I felt good and could go out. My husband would drive me downtown at around 4:00 p.m. There was always ample parking, a RARE thing in San Francisco, and we could also get into a favorite restaurant. Stores were not crowded, so we could walk around. By 5:30 or 6:00, I would get tired, and we headed home. It was the best 90 minutes of my life; I was so grateful, so present. I spent "time" anticipating these events instead of thinking about upcoming Wednesday chemo days.

Lastly, I feel it is important to include a journal entry I made prior to starting chemo.

"Been experimenting with time jumping in my thoughts. Maybe I will just "time jump" the whole chemo thing, kind of just checkout and think about what I will be doing when it's all over...well maybe better not to "time jump" the whole thing, since I might learn so much from the experience." There is no right or wrong way to do all this. You just have to experiment with what works for you.

Altering Time Exercises

I played with mindfulness awareness and altering my perception of time with some of the following exercises.

- TIME JUMP! If you have a stressful event coming up, focus on something special to do afterward and focus on that positive event instead.

- Time speed/change: On vacation and just have a few days? Slow down time awareness by being aware of all five senses as you travel through your day. Savor every taste, sight, sound, touch and smell. Slow down time in awareness and you will literally create a longer vacation experience. If you don't have any pressing schedule, put away your cell phone and hide all time devices from your sight. At first it will be hard not to try and peek. Let yourself become the device of unlimited time and enjoy resultant freedom. Let the day unfold as it will. Try this on a weekend at home as well.

- Take an art class. The powers of observation one needs to draw really will help you to slow down and to see what is before you in a miraculous way.

- Always have a buffer: Interruptions, cancelations, mistakes about scheduling are inevitable. When you build in "time" you can relax knowing that it will be a little easier to do your best that day.

- Assert yourself and SAY NO: Boy, will you have a LOT of time!!

- Insomnia: Time for breath work, stretches, meditation, head to toe body relaxation, relaxing positive memories or image replays, a sound, a trip...You fill in the blank here_____

- Cut out an hour of TV, Facebook, Twitter, etc.

LOVING-KINDNESS

The mornings I waited for the pre-operation procedures for each of my surgeries, I did breath work in the hospital while perched up in the window, mindfully watching the day awaken and unfold below me. I arrived at each surgery alone, despite my husband's concerns, so I could immerse myself in loving-kindness by using deep breaths to calm down, tune into the area around my heart and block out all thoughts, worries and expectations. In the prep room, I focused intently on those I knew and the love I felt for them and from them. I placed my hands over my heart, focusing all my energy there and gathered all my feelings of love for my friends (furry ones, too), family, and nature's beautiful miracles. Heading to the operating room, I linked my elbow to my doctor and expressed my gratitude. Then I thanked all of my doctors personally for their care. I invited all of my people, mountains, animals, trees and a river into the operation room with me. As I walked in, I literally went up towards the walls and equipment reminding myself this was just a plain old room with computers and some fancy equipment. By demystifying the room, I dialed down my fear. (Interestingly, two years later, my oncologist Dr. Chan made a video for his patients so they could view and demystify the operating room prior to surgery. I hope more doctors will use these videos.) Oh, and I also made sure I told a joke right before I went under. This insured I was laughing, and my last memories were of the surgery room staff laughing with me.

Of course, as much as I prepared myself,

I must confess that, although I used all of these techniques, some days afterward I had a mental image of me being dragged into the operating room leaving large claw-like scratch marks on the hospital floor like a terrified cartoon character. When it was over, it was okay for me to acknowledge the fear and anxiety.

After my final surgery, I started four months of chemo. As I knew the effects it would have on my body, mind, and spirit, I decided to amp up my loving-kindness practice throughout each day. When I was driving the car or walking through my day, I saturated myself with love for those who were important to me. It was as if each person or creature I sat with became a bubble of light and love lifting me up. As a result, I actually felt like Dr. Seuss's Grinch character with my heart expanding larger and larger in my chest.

Exercises for Loving-Kindness

- One of my students asked this question in class: "What if everything you thought appeared as print on your body for people to read?" Would you change your thoughts? How would you feel if you alter those thoughts to love or kindness for that person? Even your enemy?

- Focus on your heart. Place your hands on the chest where your heart is and feel love towards every person, animal, tree, sky anything that comes to mind. Bring your heart awareness and attention to this amazing universe.

- I believe words are as powerful as a slap to the face. What words do you CHOOSE to tell yourself? I call repetitive negative thoughts the "chewies". They chew up your beautiful spirit. Instead of staying with thoughts that are like corrosive acid on your body and spirit, try immediately following them with feelings/thoughts in your heart for another: the janitor or the street cleaner who keeps your area clean, people who plant seeds to grow your food, or those that pick vegetables for your grocery store. Send your thoughts to ambulance drivers or caregivers who someday may save your family or friend. Feel love for any furry, feathered, scaly, winged creature that is around you. The list is endless the possibilities for love are also.

- A powerful lesson for me: I am perfect just sitting here; I shine. You don't have to do, to go, go, go, or to make grand attempts to shine. You already shine. Find a statement that works for you expressing loving-kindness towards yourself.

- Start with the top of your head and imagine a slowly twirling double helix of light traveling down each arm, down your torso and down each of your legs.

- Make Giant Love Bombs: Intensely focus on everyone you love, feel this energy making big bubbles of support lifting you up. Just drink it in! I've spent a lot of time during difficult days immersed with the love I have for people I know and the love I feel returned from them. Giant love bombs are amazing and I want to send one now to you, Dear Reader. I hope in this moment you can feel it.

COMPASSION AND GRATITUDE

I felt lucky to have compassionate, highly-experienced nurses. However, it was also important for me not to feel like a victim or a child, but instead to be part of the team. Obviously, there were many factors I couldn't control, but I could control eating well, exercising, and meditating. After all, there was no better expert on me than me.

It was in this state of mind that I decided to bump up my own awareness of the gratitude I felt for my nurses. I thought about their day working with very ill, even terminal, patients. When I compared that to coming home from teaching, I realized that a "bad day" for me was really different than a "bad day" for chemo nurses. These nurses care for and develop relationships with patients, and often have to deal with devastating circumstances.

That was when I came upon the idea to bring an ample plate of food to the nurses. I enlisted the turkey-baking help of my husband Bill, since in my weakened state I couldn't even go grocery shopping, let alone lift a bird, and brought my nurses a large platter of delicious food when I came to chemo. This gesture was so appreciated, and ultimately so empowering for me, that I decided to try it again.

In December, I brought my nurses several bags of cones from the giant sugar pines that grow close to my cabin in the woods. They created a big holiday welcome bowl on the registration counter for all of us to enjoy, and they took some home to create hangings and other festive decor. You may be going through a life challenge that leaves you too exhausted to do this, but with your mind you can direct loving thoughts to those that care for you.

Another time my very compassionate friend, I call her Dr. Genius Gail, had an amazing collection of hats, and decided to give me twenty-five or so when she saw I was losing my hair. I knew I couldn't wear them all, so I brought some for the chemo nurses to distribute to patients throughout the day. The idea here was that they could approach patients with something other than those painful and difficult needle insertions. Their faces lit up when they saw the bags. Frankly, they were probably a little stunned as well. Then they realized the fun they would have bringing the hats to the patients. (Please clear this idea with staff. They may have strict protocols about what is allowed. You can also call the American Cancer Society for ideas about donations.)

That fall I asked Dr. Genius Gail of Reviv Med Spa if she could offer a small discount to patients and chemo nurses. Her staff printed up flyers for me to distribute offering discounts on facials. My compassionate hair stylist Lori Costabile offered a "Tuesday Super Discount" on haircuts at her salon Tease. I didn't have much control over the chemo, but distributing these flyers was great! Feeling compassion for my nurses and showing them gratitude had a side-benefit for me. I felt empowered and part of the "team," which I am convinced made me physically and mentally stronger.

Last December, I went back to the infusion center with another platter of food. The staff told me I was the only patient they could remember who ever came back voluntarily. I go back to thank them, to help reduce my own fearful memories, but mostly to bask in loving-kindness and gratitude for these amazing people.

Exercises for Compassion and Gratitude

- Wake up in the morning and notice negative thoughts or worries? Imagine a giant STOP sign. Close your eyes and think about what you want to bring to your day. Look out the window and think of someone you love. I often tell myself that there will be at least one special surprise that will happen for me each day. This exercise is very important. It allows you to program your day, to be more compassionate to yourself, to be aware of eliminating behavior you no longer wish to manifest. It begins an internal dialogue to direct behavior you can tap into throughout the day.

- Feeling sad? Do something for someone else. I keep a bag of oranges, protein bars, and warm sweaters in my car. When I run into a homeless person, I have something solid to give them. If you bustle in to an assisted-living home with energy and love, the residents' heads will turn like flowers toward the sun. Help them write and send some cards to ones they love. Once I came in with a friend in a full Victorian ball gown as I was headed to the Dickens Fair, a costume event in San Francisco. The seniors loved it, and so did we!

- Practice intense compassion for yourself every day: honoring your feelings and needs; eating healthy foods, exercising. Stop showing compassion ONLY to others and ignoring yourself.

- Honor yourself: Don't always respond right away, take a deep belly breath. Listen to your gut, and return your response at a later time if necessary. If you regret information you gave some one and you've changed your mind, honor that. Call them, and state you've changed your position.

- To do list: nap, journal, watch rainfall, lay on floor resting back muscles... your personal additions?

- Do the worst task of day first, if possible. Exhausted? Then you're done! Have to do more? Prioritize and edit your task list wherever possible. Simplify throughout your day.

- Massively congratulate yourself for each task done for the day. Extra massively congratulate yourself if you were compassionate, got rest or talked with a good friend.

- Show gratitude to those around you for what they did for you today; the smaller the gesture, the better.

- It's okay to watch a silly movie, daydream or take a break.

- Too much in one day? Ask your gut, then DROP something. Print out a bunch of complex craft projects and recipes and burn them. Then go take a walk, a nap, draw or dance around in your room.

- Can't say it enough! "Surrender" to fatigue. REST, rest, rest. One of the many things I learned from my mother-in law was to ALWAYS take a good nap. (Clearly, if you are excessively sleeping, see a specialist.)

- When you are witchy to your spouse, lover, family and you think, "Thank God, no one overheard how I sounded just now." Keep in mind, someone just did, and it was a person you love. Practice compassion every day. When you mess up, express regret, state how will you will make changes in the future, express compassion for your imperfection and commit to changing your behavior and doing better in future interactions

- To become more compassionate, we need to realize how we imprison ourselves with toxic thoughts.

- Self-made prisons of another sort: Draw yourself. Now draw wide bars over your picture. Write the words in the bars of how you imprison yourself. If you are willing to state that anything is infinitely possible, what keys would remove those bars? Write those down too.

- On a blank piece of paper draw a very large square. Imagine the square as a giant empty frame. What would freedom look like if it were in that framed space?

- Should: German word for "guilt." Enough said.

- Try out this beautiful Native American saying: There is beauty above me. There is beauty below me. There is beauty in front of me. There is beauty behind me. There is beauty all around me, and there is beauty in me.

- Remember that EVERY DAY you have the choice of which path you want to take: that of resentment and anger...or that of kindness, compassion and love. The impact of this choice affects your health, your family, the planet, and more people than you are aware. Help your reality along. Stop. Listen to your body and your thoughts. Challenge them, and choose your response.

Cushway

SHORT BURSTS OF MISERY

I worked night and day trying to stay positive. I trained for surgery/chemo like I used to train for my dance performances. I increased my breath, mindfulness, and loving-kindness work. I increased gratitude awareness and wrote daily in my journal. I continued to exercise after surgery, no matter what (power walking, Pilate floor work and free weights). I was determined not to give in to the WORD cancer or to create a total WORLD of cancer. It was just one facet of my life. Cancer did not define me. It was just something that happened to me.

It was then, while undergoing four months of chemo, I was assigned a powerhouse of a nurse practitioner to help me with both the emotional and practical aspects of having cancer. I soon named Barbara Silver my "mama bear, pit bull, enigma-therapist." She literally saved my life once and dropped a needle from 10,000 feet directly on target when she introduced me to four words. She asked me if I had ever heard of "The Prison of Positivity," a concept taught by Dr. David Spiegal of Stanford University. After our meeting, I stewed over these four words and then immediately decided I had become a prisoner in my approach to dealing with my illness.

I had focused all of my attention on being grateful for my life and engaged in the present. I fought to stay positive with every skill I had: exercise, loving-kindness, compassion, rest, diet. I watched TV when too exhausted to talk to friends on the phone, and greeted television personalities like my new

BFF's. All of this worked to a degree. In this culture, many of us maintain a kind of positivity perfectionism, and I too believe that we must bring positivity and gratitude to the table as we deal with life's events. However, I remembered people I met who tried to be Iron Woman/Man and never showed their family how awful they felt. We are not made of iron. After considering those four words, the prison of positivity, I decided that I had to acknowledge that sometimes we must surrender to our feelings of sadness, frustration, fatigue, and anger, staying with them for a while, and then move on.

I remembered trying to be stoic about losing my hair during chemo, but deep inside I was just so sad. Wasn't a woman's hair "her glory"? Didn't the French shave women's heads to humiliate them for collaborating with the enemy during World War 2? A friend of a friend, Camille, sent me a very straight forward e-mail kindly telling me to cut the stoicism and that losing your hair during chemo can be very traumatic. Her insistence freed me to feel, cry, and refocus my energies. I call it "going forward" with the caveat that sometimes we go sideways or upside down.

It was then I decided to change my management techniques for dealing with my chemo and the subsequent malfunctions that came along with it. I created 10-20 second flash flood "tune in and cry" zones to help me deal with nausea, veins collapsing, the -28 degree cold caps on my head to prevent hair loss, fatigue, and general frustration. I set aside time to be alone and allowed myself to feel just how much it hurt, how scared I felt, and how it just plain sucked to go through this.

Throughout each day, our mind-psyches are triggered by words, smells, and media images that can tap our feelings of sadness or fear. Whenever I felt these emotions, I did not question why. I just stayed with the sad, miserable feelings, but only for short bursts. I intuitively sensed when it was too much for me to continue to immerse myself in these emotions. I did not want to get stuck too long in stressful thoughts, flushing my body cells with too much angst. But I did allow myself to express and feel them.

In addition to "sitting with the sorrow" (without getting immersed in it) I used writing therapy after reading an article by Martha Beck on the subject. It was January, and I had finished chemo, but was concerned about post-traumatic stress from the past one and a half years of treatment. Designating 25 minutes a couple of times a week, I vented every sad, awful, whiney feeling I had, writing it down as fast as the thoughts flowed out of me with absolutely no judgment about what I wrote. Often these were four Kleenex or more sessions, and if this is too hard for you to do alone, you should consider working with a therapist. After 4 weeks of writing therapy, I checked in with therapist Dr. Karen Siou to make sure I was on the right path.

Loving kindness meditation, positive thinking, and mindfulness got me through surgeries, recovery and chemo. Staying in touch with the hard stressful feelings in short bursts kept me from imploding.

Exercises for Short Bursts of Misery

- You cannot go from Point A to Point C without going through Point B.

- Find a quiet place: journal, draw, or just sit and stay with what is going on in your life right now. No sugar coating. No "Oh, someone has it much worse than me." Don't just laugh about it and forget it. Stay with your truth: it hurts. It's so damn hard because right now it is exactly what you are thinking and or feeling. Have a clock to time yourself. Just feel, NO judgment, no guilt, nothing that will block the truth. Rage, cry, whatever. Start with short bursts. This is point B: uncomfortable, but one of your greatest teachers. If you can't stop crying or come out of it in 10 or 15 minutes, please seek professional help. If you cannot deal with the sad or fearful feelings, then later, in less difficult times, take the time to sit in awareness and observe what you experienced. Let it be okay to be sad, anxious, fearful. Sit with the cranky!

- Still feeling negative? Resentful? Time this exercise so you don't stay stuck. Now just sit with your cranky, whiney, resentful thoughts and clear them out of your mind/body. When I feel irritable and don't like this uncomfortable feeling, I sit with awareness and stay with the sticky feelings. Oftentimes, an awareness comes over me that I am trying to be where I am not. For example, I was sitting by a lovely river thinking I should be enjoying myself, but instead I was uncomfortable. On deeper reflection, I realized I was fighting my brain and body that wanted to discharge some thoughts into this book. I left, went to my computer and wrote for a while. Then I came back and peacefully sat by the beautiful river. Falling into the sticky moments of life provides one of our best places to learn, to choose another direction. I've made some very constructive changes in my life by sitting with my discomfort. This is usually where I find I have a buried concern. If I can allow it to bubble to the surface, then I can figure out the best solution.

- You always have a choice: Just broke your deceased grandmother's tea cup? Spilled your freshly made pot of coffee all over the counter? STOP! You can Godzilla it, turn into a screaming monster and be crazy for hours. OR do a 10-20 second anger flush: yell, jump up and down vigorously, shake your body parts, try different things that work for you to QUICKLY process through your anger, and then, "Chopra it." If you can go straight to Chopra and not have it bother you (honestly), go for it. Put on big black Deepak Chopra glasses, figuratively speaking, and try saying to yourself, "Not much really bothers me anymore." I carry these words with me and work on this all the time. In fact, I just had to practice this the other day after typing for three hours. I accidently lost all my data and had to redo the three hours of input. I sat on my couch and fussed and moaned, decided to "Chopra it," and got back to work.

- If you can't stop going on Godzilla rampages, then get a therapist and clean house. There is not one sane person on the planet. Everyone needs help of some sort.

- You have the answers you need inside you. Trisha Dodge, a grief therapist, told me this one day. I can't stress how important it is to learn to listen to your body.

- Feeling hate, resentment? Spend time feeling it. Don't stuff it down, get it out and over with. That's what swear words are for. Learn to let go and stop washing every cell in your body with acid thoughts.

- Sometimes when events are too difficult and I'm feeling overwhelmed, I try this exercise. Put your hands on the back of your neck, and gently press the neck into the hands. Be aware of that part of your body. Are you tense or rigid? When you focus on the word "Dissolve," can you sense a softening of the muscle? Try with other parts of your body: your face, your back. (Add a little loving-kindness and compassion here for each area that works so hard for you ALL day long.) Find words that work for you: melt, surrender, soften.

- When I was going through chemo and felt exhausted, I released and fell into the arms of ACCEPTANCE allowing myself to rest. To just stop. To rest. It really helped to diminish the detrimental effects of the drugs.

- Schedule a holiday weekend "comfy" night for yourself. Have an easy dinner planned and nothing else but to hang out with family, a friend or a good book.

- Some people love to be whipped into a frenzy by the holiday rush. Do you? Plan serenity days during the holidays. Visualize them. Make them happen by scheduling these breaks in your calendar.

- It's okay to hate having houseguests. Some people love it; you don't have to.

- Went through a horrible stressful event? Feel like after it's all over, you have just been dumped out of a chute?   Just consider that this is a new beginning. There are an infinite number of possibilities that may manifest themselves. Something really good could be around the corner.

EXERCISE REGULARLY

Regular exercise burns up stress hormones like adrenaline and cortisol that can ravage your body. In turn, exercise promotes the feeling of wellbeing. It produces norepinephrine, serotonin, dopamine and gamma-amino butyric acid (a neurotransmitter that actually SLOWS down the transmissions between your nerve cells). Exercise not only prolongs your life, but it could save your life. I am positive it helped to save mine.

Several hours after a blood draw though my pic line (a catheter inserted in my body), I was driving home from a 4:00 p.m. meeting with my "pit bull" NP Barb Silver. I was on my headset phone telling my husband that I felt funny, like I was getting a migraine. I drove through the San Francisco hills, taking an extremely steep one-way street against my husband's advice. For once, this turned out to be a very good thing. As I crested the top of a hill, I looked up, saw white sparkling lights in the sky, and that is all I remember. My car, apparently, went straight down the hill, turned, and crashed tilted upwards on top of a water fountain in a little landscaped garden area just off the street. The next memory I have is coming to with a young man banging on my window to see if I was all right. Disoriented, I looked down and realized I was covered from waist to mid-calf in my own vomit. I told him to back away as I shook and threw up again, feeling excruciating muscle pain in my thighs and back. My headset had fallen to the passenger side, and my husband was listening to strange sounds wondering what was going on. Thankfully, the young man came back to care for me. Disoriented, I gave him the phone, and he described my location to my husband. (I have never seen that young man since but send him loving thoughts of gratitude whenever the memories resurface.) Figuring I had only a few minutes before I would pass out again, I called the tow company. Eventually they arrived, along with my husband and the fire department. They all stood around shaking their heads, amazed at how I could have landed as safely as I did, and even more so, that the fountain still worked. I got home, and after a few hours, I was shaken up and exhausted, but okay. I thought I had a severe migraine attack or food poisoning.

The next day, Wednesday, white as a ghost, I still made it to the infusion center. As soon as I was given the pre-chemo drugs, I lost muscular control and every part of my body began shaking uncontrollably. Terrified, I closed my eyes and reached for one thing I knew could help me, my breath. The nurses administered Demerol which did not work fast enough, so again, I applied a breath exercise. I put my tongue on the roof of my mouth behind my front teeth and breathed. BOOM! I slowed down.

In order to discover what had caused my body to go into rigors, the nurses took blood from the arm with the pic line and my other arm. Everything was apparently okay. I even received a phone call the next morning from the doctor's office stating I could leave for a weekend trip to the mountains. For some strange reason, my husband, who never checks our landline phone, checked the answering service right before we headed out the door. My "pit bull" Barb Silver had done it again. Her message said to drop everything and get to the Emergency Room immediately. My results had come back from the blood tests. My pic line had indeed given me blood sepsis poisoning, and I should have been hospitalized after the car crash. When I arrived at the ER, the doctor was amazed at how lucid I was. She said that by rights she should be hospitalizing me for the night, but when they did a new blood test, they couldn't believe what they saw. I had the white blood cell count of a healthy person, not even a chemo patient, results that were completely different than two days before. I was released to go home that night. I emphatically believe that the results could have been much worse, if not catastrophic, had I not been exercising pre-surgery, post-surgery and during chemo.

As to the crash, I have driven that street several times now and have no idea how my car drove itself straight downhill, avoiding vehicles parked on both sides, only to make a detour into a safe landscaped area.

So, exercise is a requirement. Out of shape, or recovering from illness? Make a bargain with yourself to walk just 10 minutes one way. Then you only have 10 minutes to get back! Can't do 10 minutes? Try 5. Or try just a few stretches. After my third surgery, I panted over to the first street sign, and then waddled to the next one. Sometimes that was all I could do. The main thing is I got out and walked.

Exercises for Exercise

- If you are close to shopping areas, walk for errands that don't require heavy bags. Wear a back pack (I use a super lightweight one), or get a back pack with wheels to make the return trip easier. Save bus fare or gas and parking, get a cardio workout, and get your errands done. Always keep some money with you in case you can't make the return home.

- As your stamina increases, lengthen distance and exertion level. I have walked all the way across San Francisco, checking out new stores, meeting new people and noticing new things I would never have seen while driving.

- Make your fitness walk your outdoor office. Keep a pen and pad handy so you can make lists. Return phone calls while you walk. The phone calls keep me so busy I don't notice I am working out. This is an especially good time to catch up with those really "chatty" friends.

- Can't walk? Do upper body cardio: chair or bed dancing, move your arms and hands. Exercise because you love yourself and want to be a good caretaker of this incredible vessel that you inhabit!

- Exercise/No excuses: Just as the stewardess tells you to reach for your oxygen mask first, then assist with your child's mask, so too you need to ensure your own exercise, rest, nourishment and fun.

- Change what type of cardio exercise you do to keep your muscles challenged and to stay interested in all of your exercise activities.

- Know when to slow down: If you are extremely anxious and wound up, don't proceed with your intense cardio workout. Sometimes it can exacerbate the problem. Take a stretch, yoga, or Pilates class instead. Let your body recoup and SLOW down.

STAY IN TOUCH WITH THE ABSURD

Laughter got me through the last section of a very difficult time with my chemo infusion. After the blood sepsis poisoning events, the floodgates opened and my body's immune system went downhill. I contracted a severe case of shingles with sciatic nerve pain in my right leg so bad it hurt to sit, lie down, or stand. I could only put weight on my left leg. The nerves in my right foot were so sensitive that it hurt if anything brushed against the skin. The shingles covered a good part of the right side of my lower back, as well as the back and inside of my leg down to my knee. The bumps connected together into raised, blue-black welts. Two doctors saw me, and both of them physically winced. My oncologist decided I should skip one chemo session.

Meanwhile, my husband contracted a cold, and guess what? Yours truly, with shingles and not able to miss another chemo session, came down with a cold! I was confined to total bed rest and had never been so miserable in my life.

Too congested to do my breathing exercises, let alone walk or pump iron, I decided I was going to fight instead by going into "positivity high drive." I flooded my body cells with love and laughter to try and heal enough to finish my chemo. I literally pasted a smile on my face, shambling around my house in my robe. I balanced this with phone calls to girlfriends and super sister-in-law Terry, not holding back one bit in my whining and complaining just to get those frustrated feelings out.

The trick was I didn't stay in the frustrated mental state. I watched anything on television that even hinted at being funny, anything that had a chance of making me laugh, even a fake one. I'll never forget one difficult Monday belly-laughing at an oversized reindeer called "Dancer" sashaying across the screen with bits of its costume falling here and there and the occasional Christmas bulb crashing down from its antlers. Someday I want to hug that darn reindeer. I truly believe that my pasted on smile and those goofy programs helped me make it to my last chemo session.

Plastering a smile on your face in the privacy of your own home is so healing, but you don't need to smile at people who dare to pronounce their judgments about serious problems or illness to you. Please, just run like hell! I can't stand it when people intimate that somehow I need a lesson from my illness.

"Why did you get cancer?" they will say. Or, "What did you need to learn?" I don't believe that God or the universe selects me or a five-year-old girl with leukemia to learn something from disease. I'll repeat here, stuff happens. Of course, we can learn from anything in our journey through life. If you can take the good AND the bad to learn new things, to make different choices for your life, then you benefit from all that happens to you. In fact, I would not even assign good or bad titles. We do not choose to suffer terribly, but when a storm ravages through the woods some trees are uprooted, and some lose branches. That is just how it works.

Cancer was part of the reality road I had to travel. I have learned not to take my reality personally, because EVERY TIME I have fought my reality, I lost. Reality always wins. Stuff happens! You can fight your reality, cry and moan, exhaust yourself, raise your blood pressure and stress yourself out to scary degrees. In the end, whatever is happening in your life is still there. It all comes down to HOW you handle it. I remember reading a quote from a Navy Seal in *O Magazine* who had immersed himself in mindfulness work. He said, when things are going well and you do your practice, it's easy. The trick is how you cope when things are bad. I decided to be a bad ass Navy Seal as well. In order to do that, I have to practice when life is going well so I'm ready for the winds and storms later.

I want to emphasize that it is so important that we do not compare how we each deal with trauma and who is suffering more. There are so many factors: age, experience, mentoring and body types. Just stay present with what you are dealing with, experiment with your new coping methods, and discover what works for you.

Exercises for Staying in Touch with the Absurd:

- Find ways to ignore those who want to try to make meaning out of your situation.

- Exercise smiling, laughing and or just being goofy.

- Cliff Jumping: I have always been a cliff jumper and taken chances with my life, like writing this book. Your life change idea may seem crazy to you at first, and you may be in free fall for a while, but you definitely will land in a new place.

- Paste a smile on your face. Just observe the feelings you have when you smile.

- Read, watch amusing stuff, tell jokes, find what works for you. Take a chance and do something that feels a little, well, absurd. NO judgments here. Everyone has different ideas of what is humorous.

- Observe others. Pay attention to how they make you feel. Who makes you smile and laugh? Negative friends and family that steal your light go to the back of the bus, and some eventually will have to get off the bus. Enemies aren't worth the energy and time they consume. Practice letting go. Direct your thoughts to a fantastic memory, person, or place, and spend some time there instead.

- Love those people that treat you well and deserve your love. Don't deserve your love? Stop giving it endlessly away and find those that do.

- Expectations? Fill in a holiday here_____. See yellow

flashing warning lights! This can be a huge black hole of crazy thoughts and negativity. Maybe you only have 20 to zero more holiday celebrations, birthdays? Maybe only one wedding day. Do you really want to go on a Godzilla Rampage and burn this one up?

- Listen to your thoughts. What are you telling yourself? Challenge your preconceived ideas, open a gazillion more doors, travel through some of them. A gazillion more may open. They may very well take you in directions you never dreamed of before.

- Do you really need that expensive kitchen gadget, pair of pants or dress? Especially if you can't afford it? What about debt, emergency cash cushion, stress? Does anyone REALLY need to buy more stuff? There is something

really weird about the amount of junk
we can purchase.

THE ELEPHANT IN THE ROOM: SEX! TO DO OR NOT TO DO

I pondered whether or not to include this topic. In addition to being very personal, it could be a whole book in itself. Upon reflection, I feel my husband and I have made discoveries that could help a lot of people. As we go through stressful events, illness, pregnancy, loss, injury and just plain old age, our sexual abilities, needs and desires change. One thing that drives me crazy is when people say "Well, you just have to get used to the new normal." What the hell does that really mean? There is, in truth, no "normal." Normal does not exist if you mean that everything in your life should be constant. We are evolving, changing creatures. Normal is what is happening in the present moment, not how things were a month ago, five years ago, or how they will be a year from now. My plan is to keep rediscovering how to work with this present moment, with these conditions that I'm given. I would like to share that process and history with you.

Four years prior to my cancer diagnoses, my husband was diagnosed with a very aggressive form of prostate cancer, level four, requiring immediate action.

His prostate was radiated, and he has had five subsequent radiations for metastasized cancer on various parts of his body. He receives four androgen deprivation shots a year to block testosterone, the hormone cancer uses to grow, with additional daily pills to block any possibility of his body producing testosterone. The result of all this is an inability to get a full erection and lack of libido.

After his initial diagnosis, radiation, and damage to his sexual organs, we met with a young doctor who told us he had 4-7 months to live. We left shattered. To handle his various medications, he was put on a high dose of prednisone which changed his personality. The initial diagnosis, radiation, body damage, and hormone blockage depressed and stressed him; the high-dose prednisone made this normally very low-keyed, easy-going guy into a nervous, irritable, hyper and anxious one. I found I could no longer reach him. He was shut down and parts of me were shutting down too.

Prior to all this, we were a sexually intimate, loving couple, unusually close and best friends. After his cancer treatment, we no longer had any intimacy. He would joke to friends over the phone, "Sex, honestly? I could care less." Hurt and confused, I asked one of his doctors about sexual intimacy. The doctor tried to disguise his discomfort and suggested sexy magazines. That's it? We are just going to look at *Playboy*?!

After a year of frustration, I decided to tackle our problems step by step. I met with his doctors about his personality change, and they agreed to reduce his prednisone. In addition, we went on long drives together where I would read to him my class lectures and review all the information I was learning about mindfulness, reframing one's thinking, meditation, loving-kindness and gratitude. He told me it was making a difference in his day to day ability to deal with his illness and life's general stress.

Realizing once again I was a prisoner of my preconceived perceptions, I decided to reframe our intimate connection. Rather than no intimacy at all, I could at least give my husband a naked woman to hold and touch. We could slow down and try other things.

I went to a tiny back section of a clothing store in a small town called Grass Valley that is near our vacation home in the mountains. I talked to a very young woman around twenty years old about some of the merchandise, various types of stuff for sexual enhancement. My education was just getting started. I bought silky, tactile lingerie clothing and some interesting toys. The toys sometimes brought about an erection; and although it couldn't be maintained, it was getting blood flow to the area and giving him confidence for the future. However, now I had a problem. When a woman has not been penetrated for several years (or has hormonal changes, or had an accident, or various surgeries), her vaginal wall thins and shrinks. This can make traditional sex very painful or impossible. I thought, "Well, that's it. Nothing is ever going in there again!"

Then came my diagnosis with cancer: surgery in April, a D&C, a full hysterectomy, and a subsequent third surgery in June. The last thing on my mind was SEX! I felt I would never have the chance of any kind of intimacy with my husband again. I couldn't even think about my pelvic area.

In mid-July, I called a very dear friend from a dance company many lifetimes ago, Pilates body worker Cindy Brain. Over the phone we diagnosed some of these problems. I realized I was over protective of my pelvis, contracting forward in a semi-fetal position, no longer standing up straight. It was as if I were preparing for an imminent attack. Cindy encouraged me to breathe into my pelvic area, to reconnect as a dancer with that area, and to place my hands on the front of my hips and gently push forward as I walked in order to gradually straighten up. It worked! I progressed on to my stretching regimen and started preparing myself for chemo starting mid-August.

Enter NP "pit-bull" Barb Silver again. After telling her my concerns, she told me about Dr. Laura Berman's Dilator set, a product with several sizes designed to gradually open the vaginal wall, train muscles, and strengthen the pelvic floor. It also has a "vibratory option to take the clinical edge off dilator use by making the focus on pleasure as well as training" I knew this knowledge was a harbinger of hope and filed it away until I felt well enough to explore the option.

God bless Laura Berman! The woman is a genius if you as a woman are having the troubles I described, put this book down and go order her set immediately!

Don't be afraid to do some exploration on your own. In San Francisco, where I permanently reside, I went to Good Vibrations, a store that sells sex toys. There I met with more well-informed twenty-year-olds who talked frankly with me about how various tools could be used for people of both sexes who have health issues. I had a LOT to learn from these young people! One staff member explained that even though a man is hormone deprived, his brain is still engaged and that thrusting motions are important to the male sexual psyche. I bought the rabbit vibrator (Check out the *Sex in the City* rabbit intervention episode) and a Guybrator for my husband.

Keeping the blood flowing to his penis means he has a better chance of sexual functioning if (and when) there are medical advancements for prostrate patients. I am older and plumper, but in pretty lingerie with the lights down REALLY low (okay, off) I think I'm a pretty hot cookie. My brain knows that these toys will give me pleasure; his brain knows that too. This positive reinforcement has meant more intimate encounters, sometimes just mindfully holding each other. Plus, we go through our day feeling glad we still have each other. These tools/toys are amazing, and although we aren't where we used to be, that is just how life is. You are never where you used to be! Lastly, I know there is a whole slow sex movement out there that discourages vibrators, but frankly, we don't have time to worry about that. It's use it or lose it.

Exercises for The Elephant in the Room

- Go shopping.

- Okay, go online if you can't get to a store. However, going to a brick and mortar store is better because the staff knows about the products and can individualize what might be best for you or just plain fun to try.

- Please purchase the dilator set from Laura Berman per your doctor's advice. I can't advocate this strongly enough. Take your time with the progressive additions. Go back down in size if you've had any urinary tract or vaginal infections.

- Cuddling is great. I just had lunch with a couple who met on the first day of high school and are now 80 years old!! You should see those two rave about cuddling together at night. Plan TIME just to hang out and talk with your partner, with no expectations other than to focus on one another and just BE.

SURVIVING AND THRIVING

My oncologist required three month check-ups post chemo. After the first visit, my doctor expressed how really happy he was with my results. When I asked him why, he stated "Because you have made it through 3 months, and the serous cancer was the one I was worried about. The odds weren't in your favor" It has been two years since that day, and I have graduated to six month checkups.

During chemo, the cold caps preserved

maybe half of my hair. However, three months post chemo, it started falling out again until I had only one third of my hair and the frightening possibility that I would be bald forever. I sat myself down and, with great difficulty and hard work, came to terms with this fact, moving towards acceptance of my permanent hair loss and surrendering to this new reality. Immersed in gratitude and mindfulness, I rebooted my brain to concentrate not on hair loss, but on the wonderful fact that I was plump, sassy and very much alive. However, my hair has grown back thick and full, utilizing the scientifically researched and developed organic products, strict methodology and counseling provided by Dr. Erkkie Harris-Wells. Within two weeks of beginning her hair treatment, my hair stopped falling out.

I teach intense Cardio Dance classes

with head to toe body strengthening exercises. My students range from 17 to 60 years old, and I can out move those 17 year olds, well most of them. I walk on days I don't teach and keep up my regimen of weights, push ups, and floor work when on summer break. I feel stronger and have more energy than I had three or four years prior to surgeries and chemo.

Although I still have recurrent back pain, I've learned to work with our campus physical trainer on ankle/body alignment and strength. I choose mindful awareness of the day around me instead of focusing on the pain. Each six-month exam could bring results that the cancer has returned. Prior to testing, I pay attention to levels of anxiety, acknowledge them, and then shift my thinking. It is not easy! I work hard to stay with what I have now and guide my thoughts to deal with the future when it comes. I have to practice breath work, gratitude, and mindfulness every day, because when I get busy and forget, I lose all of the beautiful and meaningful lessons I have learned in my life's journeys. My husband still requires four androgen deprivation shots a year, and takes daily pills to block hormones. He was scheduled for his sixth radiation session four months ago. They canceled it, as they couldn't find the tumor. His blood work revealed that the cancer is no longer detectable. We realize he is not cured. When the medication is no longer efficacious, the cancer will reproduce, but for now, we have a good chance that he may make it until a new drug or treatment is available.

SOME FINAL THOUGHTS

Check out lectures, books, and blogs on the latest in neuroscience. It will rock your world, explaining how our bodies work physiologically and cognitively. Find a magazine, blog or book that changes your awareness and try to read something from it every day to stay plugged in to yourself and the world around you. Share your discoveries with friends and family. When you make poor choices, you feed the fires of shame and increase the negative feelings. Work on forgiving yourself instead.

Christianity, Judaism, Hinduism, AA meetings, scientific investigation - it doesn't matter what road you choose, as long as it plugs you in and connects you to the wonder of our universe/multiverse. For me, reading about quantum mechanics was instrumental in opening up my tiny little world.

I recently read a fun book that stated magic is all around us, and the thought made me feel so good I decided to make it my reality. In our lives, the concept of magic is transcendent and lifts us into the swirling mysteries and mind blowing awesomeness of the world. So much of what is possible today would be considered magic in past centuries. Harry Potter's "magic invisibility cloak" is actually a scientific construct today. Scientists have found a way to refract light from an object, rendering it invisible to an observer. Whether religion, science, or magic, the power of mystery and something greater than ourselves can help us verify our own unique magnificence.

Gene Roddenberry, creator of the *Star Trek* film series, referred to the spaceship Enterprise as a metaphor for the planet earth. I marvel that, indeed, I am traveling on a huge "ship" orbiting a giant star, part of a galaxy, in a universe that extends to infinity, and potentially part of an infinite number of universes. Friends often remark about how looking at the universe makes them feel that their problems are small, which is one way of looking at things. I, however, think about the smallness of quarks or the Higgs Bosen particle when compared to the vastness of the infinite universe, and marvel that I fit in between those extremes and am part of the whole picture. I sit here writing this to you, knowing that I exist in this vast unbelievable magical world, and by association, I am a magical being. That thought makes me smile as I stand in gratitude and awe of what is around me that I can and cannot see.

Stop Choose Change

ACKNOWLEDGMENTS

Thank you to my fantastic editor, Irene Frazier. I could feel this book slipping away from me and firmly believe it would never have come to fruition had I not found you to edit it. Mary Johnsen , you insisted Irene and I meet for lunch so we could get to know each other before you moved. Wow, were you ever right. How did you know? Best sister-in-law ever, Terry, thanks for your patient listening through all of my toughest times. Loving thanks to my Aunt Esther, one of my greatest mentors. Dr. Karen Siou, one of my greatest teachers. Thanks to Ellen Johnson for suggestions on editing and recommending that I slow down and really work on structure. Virgil, you cheered me on before I even started typing! Thanks to Bradley Charbonneau for pushing me and creating the book's website. Angela, part of Bradley's team, thank you for editing and page layout for the ebook, creating the sales page, recommending book cover designers, assisting with last minute problems and lastly, for holding my hand - you pushed me to the finish line! Molly Ortega for invaluable advice on all aspects of producing this book and her contributions in the final book layout and editing. Rich and Liz, thanks for letting me work at your kitchen table and read to you rough draft selections. Special thanks to: Dr. Natasha Curry for your humor, compassion and devotion; Jan Fosberg for being so fantastically awesome; Marie Norris - you are a gem. My hardworking cold cap session caretakers: Sue Abuzeide, Ercie Santos, Cindy Brain, Kayla Rae Madison (Cushway), Deb Mondro, (Deb, your feedback gave me the confidence to keep writing). My gratitude goes to Dr. Gail Riesly, for your unbelievable compassion, generosity with discounts for cancer patients and staff, and especially your brilliant mind. I will never forget the day, sometime after my third surgery, I stopped by to say hi to you. I looked and felt like hell. You took one look at me and ordered your staff to bundle me up for a warm blanket spa treatment. Wow, it was SO rejuvenating. Frank Lang at the Downieville clinic, you so rock! Dr. Chan, my oncologist, thanks for saving my life. Lori Costabile, I deeply appreciate you for your salon discounts for medical staff and cancer patients, not to mention some very good advice. Jose Bonilla, your information and help on back problems enabled me to keep writing. Dr. Erkkie Harris-Wells of Miyohara International (Hair Loss Clinic), you are utterly amazing (my hair did grow back and it is unbelievable!) Ann, you were truly a gift for me! NP Barb Silver, thank you for developing and running the awesome women's center. My endless gratitude to my wonderful mentor, Dr.

Karen Siou. Thank you Trisha Dodge, you told me that I was a million miles ahead of myself and that eventually I would catch up. I believe I have! To all my friends, family and colleagues that I haven't listed, I am so grateful to have you in my life! Big thanks to my husband Bill for listening, checking initial drafts, rescuing me from the monster computer, and supporting me throughout my writing process. My exploding heartfelt thanks to my mother and father in law Bill and Dorothy Evans for all the love and support that they gave me. Bill, I cherish you and love the way you cherish me, you are my rock.

Stop Choose Change

Cushway

ABOUT THE AUTHOR

Diana Cushway is a professor in the Kinesiology, Dance and Athletics Department at Skyline College in San Bruno, California. As the former head of Skyline's Dance Department, she expanded faculty and curriculum in addition to producing sold out concerts. She was an early advocate of incorporating mindfulness and breath practice into her classroom to help her students deal with stress. Her success in this endeavor led her to develop a stress management curriculum and teach classes at the college level.

Diana has been a California Arts Council Grant recipient in Bay Area schools, a guest artist throughout the US, and a dancer and/or choreographer for many Bay Area modern dance companies.

In remission after surviving two

simultaneous cancer diagnoses, she currently lives (surviving and thriving) in San Francisco with her husband, Bill, and her one cat, Butterflopper.

The author is available for lectures/workshops to expand on information in this book.

49243237R00079

Made in the USA
San Bernardino, CA
17 May 2017